Sweet Sixteen

16 REASONS WHY YOU'RE AMAZING

"The most effective
way to do it,
is to do it."

-AMELIA EARHEART

Reason #1

"You are enough.
Just the way you are.
Just who you are."

Reason #2

"It is better to conquer yourself than to win a thousand battles.
Then the victory is yours."

-BUDDHA

Reason #3

"I have not failed.
I've just found 10,000
ways that don't work."

-THOMAS EDISON

Reason #4

"The other girls?
They've got nothing on you."

-ANONYMOUS

Reason #5

"The best way to
predict the future
is to create it."

-ABRAHAM LINCOLN

Reason #6

"Beauty is created by your attitude, your behaviour & your actions."

-ANONYMOUS

Reason #7

"Happiness and confidence are the prettiest things you can wear."

-TAYLOR SWIFT

Reason #8

"Always be a first rate version of yourself, instead of a second rate version of someone else."

-JUDY GARLAND

Reason #9

"Courage doesn't always roar. Sometimes courage is the quiet voice at the end of the day saying, "I will try again tomorrow."

-MARY A RADMACHER

Reason #10

"The difference between winning and losing is most often not quitting."

-WALT DISNEY

Reason #11

"No one can make you feel inferior without your consent."

-ELEANOR ROOSEVELT

Reason #12

"Always chase your dreams instead of running from your fears."

-ANONYMOUS

Reason #13

"Believe in yourself
and you can do
unbelieveable things."

-ANONYMOUS

Reason #14

"When someone tells you
that you can't, turn
around and say
'watch me'."

-ANONYMOUS

Reason #15

"And though she
may be little,
she is fierce."

-WILLIAM SHAKESPEARE

Reason #16

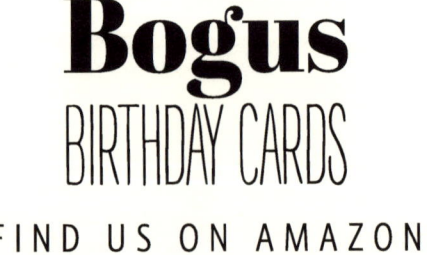

Made in the USA
Coppell, TX
07 February 2023

12317771R00021